TRA
HORS

Transporting Horses by Road

THRESHOLD BOOKS
THE BRITISH HORSE SOCIETY

Text by John Bullock
Edited by Judith Draper and David Harding
Designed by The Graphic Partnership

© 1986 Threshold Books Ltd

Produced in association with the
British Horse Society by
Threshold Books Limited,
661 Fulham Road, London SW6 5PZ.

The publishers and the British Horse Society
acknowledge with thanks the help given with
the text by the Road Transport Industry
Training Board and with the illustrations by
Avonride Ltd, Indespension Ltd, Lambourn
Coachbuilders Ltd and Rice Trailers Ltd.

Phototypeset by Falcon Graphic Art Ltd,
Wallington, Surrey
Printed by Guernsey Press, Guernsey, CI

ISBN 0 901366 04 8

Contents

Trailers, Horseboxes and the New Regulations

The need to transport horses quickly and safely by road has led to the development of both the horse trailer, which can be towed behind another vehicle, and the horsebox, which is mounted on a commercial vehicle chassis and moves under its own power. These two types of vehicle are necessarily treated differently by the law in many respects, and also require a different approach from the user. This book seeks to provide the information a user will need to run either type safely and legally on the roads of the United Kingdom and Europe.

A British user of a horse trailer or a horsebox may be affected by United Kingdom laws or EEC laws, according to the circumstances. In recent years new Common Market regulations have been introduced which affect anyone transporting horses in Europe. These regulations have caused changes in the design, maintenance and use of trailers and horseboxes, and have considerably improved the safety factors. The regulations will be explained at each stage of the book, as relevant to the particular topic under discussion.

Horse Trailers

Trailers are usually designed to transport one, two or three horses or ponies, and to be towed by a relatively light vehicle. Although all trailers have a parking brake for use when stationary, some have no braking system of their own for use when in motion, and rely entirely on the brakes of the towing vehicle. Under the new regulations there are restrictions on the comparative weights of an unbraked trailer and its towing vehicle.

Types of Trailer

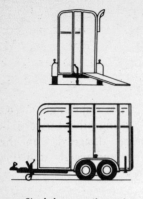 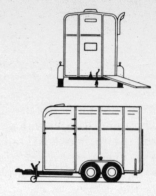

Single horse trailer with
rear and side ramps.

Double horse trailer, also with side unload.

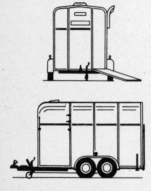 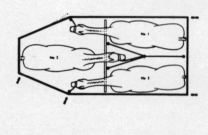

Trailer designed to carry three horses, two facing the front, one facing the rear.

The majority of one- and two-horse trailers are designed for the animals to travel in forward-facing stalls, with a ramp at the rear and sometimes a side ramp for unloading. Some trailers, however, are designed for the horses to face the rear, and it is important to ensure that they face the correct way, or the balance of the trailer during towing may be seriously affected.

Although some trailers are mounted on a single two-wheel axle, the majority have two axles and four wheels mounted in what is termed 'close coupled' formation. This means that both wheels on one side of a trailer travel parallel to the longitudinal axis, rather than being steered. The distance between the points where the tyres make contact with the road must be a maximum of one metre.

Motorised Horseboxes

The motorised horsebox offers more options and greater flexibility than a trailer, and has thus been steadily gaining in popularity among horse owners and trainers. It will usually carry more horses than a trailer, and may also incorporate living accommodation for the driver and passengers. There is no restriction on the number of passengers who may be carried in a horsebox, although none may travel in a trailer.

The stalls for the horses may be arranged at right angles across the horsebox, or diagonally with the animals facing either forwards or backwards. More horseboxes are now being designed with this diagonal arrangement, because it saves space and weight and thus allows for a substantial amount of living accommodation — something especially sought after in horseboxes of up to 7.5 tonnes gross vehicle weight, which can be driven on a normal car licence.

Anyone wishing to drive a horsebox will need to check the legally permitted maximum weight of the vehicle and its load combined ('gross vehicle weight'), as this is the major factor in determining the minimum age and qualifications of the driver and the need or otherwise for a tachograph, log book, Heavy Goods Vehicle Licence and Operator's Licence.

Accidents involving horse transport are unfortunately all too common. It is hoped that this book will enable the reader to move horses by road with the maximum safety and in full compliance with the law.

Chapter 1

The Trailer and its Systems

General

The new trailer regulations bring the United Kingdom more in line with the EEC regulations already in use in many other European countries, and are an important move towards ensuring the safety of all new trailers and their occupants.

The driver is held responsible for the vehicle and its load and therefore must make sure that everything is secured both on and in the vehicle and trailer. He would be open to prosecution if anything should fall on to the roadway and cause danger to other road users.

The normal maximum permitted length for a trailer is 7m and horse trailers are usually well within that dimension. The trailer must not be more than 2.3m at its widest point, and horse trailers are again usually well within this limit. They are, however, frequently wider than the towing vehicle, and that is why they are subject to special regulations, such as the positioning of the front corner lights, and the use of extra mirrors on the towing vehicle.

All trailers must have an adequate mudguard on each wheel except where the design of the body provides adequate protection. They must also have a rear number plate showing the same registration number as the towing vehicle.

Vehicles registered on or after 1 January 1973, and the trailers which they tow, must have reflex reflecting number plates showing white to the front and yellow to the rear. In both cases the letters and the numbers must be in black. The plates should carry the mark 'B.S. AU 145:1967' or 'B.S. AU 145a:1971'.

Examples of trailer couplings and braking systems

Avonride axles with auto reverse brakes used in conjunction with Bradley MK10 coupling

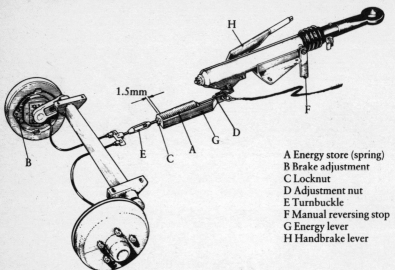

A Energy store (spring)
B Brake adjustment
C Locknut
D Adjustment nut
E Turnbuckle
F Manual reversing stop
G Energy lever
H Handbrake lever

Avonride axles with auto reverse brakes used in conjunction with Bradley coupling

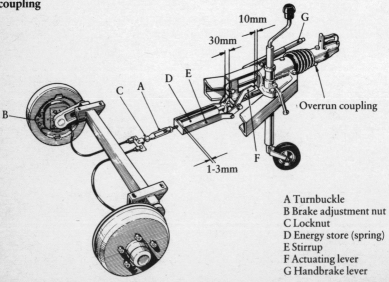

A Turnbuckle
B Brake adjustment nut
C Locknut
D Energy store (spring)
E Stirrup
F Actuating lever
G Handbrake lever

Examples of trailer couplings and braking systems

**Avonride axles and coupling used
with standard rod operated brakes**

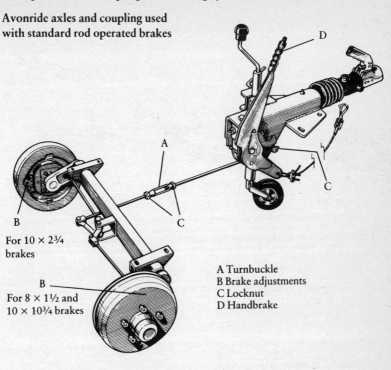

For 10 × 2¾
brakes

For 8 × 1½ and
10 × 10¾ brakes

A Turnbuckle
B Brake adjustments
C Locknut
D Handbrake

**Avonride axles and coupling used
with auto reverse brakes**

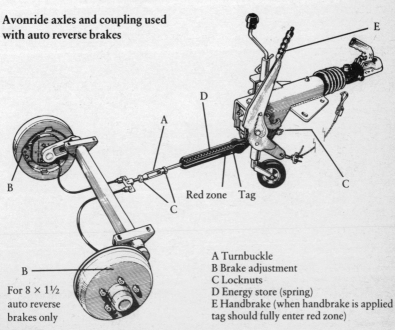

Red zone   Tag

For 8 × 1½
auto reverse
brakes only

A Turnbuckle
B Brake adjustment
C Locknuts
D Energy store (spring)
E Handbrake (when handbrake is applied
tag should fully enter red zone)

Brakes

Dealing first with trailers which do not have their own full braking system, it is now permissible to construct and use an unbraked trailer with a gross weight of up to 750kg (15cwt). This means that brakes are not needed where the gross weight of the trailer is 750kg or less.

All unbraked trailers must be marked in a readily visible place with their maximum gross weight (in kilograms). The nearside of the tow-bar is the place most often chosen, and the weight may be painted on without the need for any special label or plate. Some trailers will have a gross weight of less than 750kg depending on the limitations of suspension, wheels and tyres. It is now an offence to load a trailer above its maximum gross weight.

The towing vehicle must weigh at least twice as much as a new trailer when loaded and therefore it is important to know the weight of your towing vehicle. As a general guide, a petrol engined Land-Rover has a kerb weight of approximately 1380kg, which means that it would be unable to tow an unbraked trailer of more then 690kg, but a Range-Rover weighing 1782kg could tow a trailer up to the maximum weight of 750kg.

As for trailers with brakes, the braking system of new trailers must now comply with EEC directive 71/320, which means that the trailer must be fitted with hydraulically damped over-run couplings with correctly matched brakes and linkage instead of the old spring-operated type. The combination of vehicle and trailer must also have a minimum braking efficiency of 45% G.

Although these new laws apply at present only to trailers manufactured after 1 October 1982, owners may wish to modify their older trailers for safety reasons. From 1 October 1986 the laws will apply to trailers of any age.

All trailers, of whatever type and age, must be equipped with a parking brake (capable of being operated by a person standing on the ground) which will hold the trailer fully laden on a gradient of 1 in 6.25.

Reversing Clip

Braked trailers with over-run couplings usually have a reversing clip, which must be fixed on before attempting to reverse with the trailer coupled to the towing vehicle. Failure to apply the clip will cause the brakes to be applied as the vehicle pushes back against the coupling, thus hindering reversing and possibly damaging the trailer. However, many newer trailers now have a 'reversing brake system' which avoids the problem automatically, without the driver needing to get out and fix on a clip.

Breakaway Cable

A safety device called a 'breakaway cable' is advisable, as it will help bring the trailer to a halt should it ever break away from the towing vehicle on the road. It consists of a noose of steel cable attached to the trailer, which you loop over the hook on the towing vehicle. Should the coupling fail and the trailer break away from the towing vehicle, before the breakaway cable snaps, it will be pulled tight by the hook and will automatically apply the brakes to bring the runaway trailer to a standstill.

Tyres

The regulations applying to the tyres fitted to motor vehicles also apply to trailer tyres. There are two types, cross ply and radial ply, and under no circumstances may a mixture of different types be fitted on the same axle. It is recommended that the same type of tyre should be fitted on the towing vehicle and the trailer, but it is permissible to have one type of tyre on the towing vehicle and another on the trailer. If, for example, the towing vehicle has cross ply tyres on the front and radial ply tyres on the rear, either type may be fitted to the trailer, although by mixing types the stability and control may be reduced.

Every pneumatic tyre fitted to a motor vehicle or trailer must comply with the following rules:

It must be suitable for the use to which the vehicle or trailer is being put.

It must be correctly inflated.

It must be free from any cut which is deep enough to reach the body cords and is in excess of 22mm or 10% of the tyre section width, whichever is the greater.

It must be free from any lump, bulge or tear caused by separation or partial failure of its structure.

It must be free from scrubbing or damage so extensive that the cord or ply is exposed.

The base of any groove which formed part of the original tread pattern must be clearly visible (i.e. any baldness is illegal).

The grooves of the tread pattern of the tyre must have a depth of at least 1mm throughout a continuous band measuring at least three-quarters of the breadth of the tread and round its entire circumference.

Some types of tyre are designed to operate safely when deflated. They must carry an identification mark on the outside walls.

Lights

The Motor Vehicle Lighting Regulations stipulate the minimum size and number of lights which must be fitted to all road vehicles, including trailers. They also specify the colours, minimum and maximum wattages, and the dimensions within which the lights must be fitted. Trailer manufacturers naturally comply with all these regulations when constructing trailers for sale to the public for use on public roads. But when carrying out alterations or repairs oneself, the specifications laid down in the manufacturer's handbook should be carefully followed.

Trailer light positions

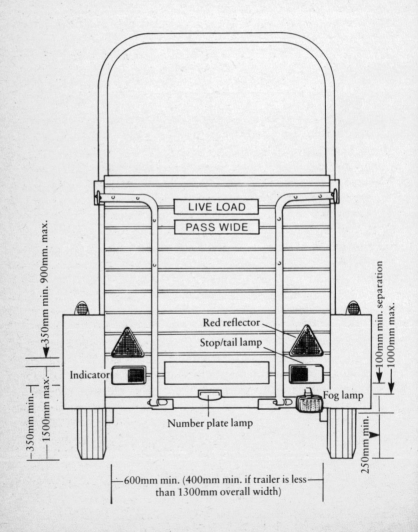

LIVE LOAD

PASS WIDE

350mm min. 900mm. max.

Red reflector

Stop/tail lamp

Indicator

350mm min.

1500mm max.

100mm min. separation

1000mm max.

Fog lamp

Number plate lamp

250mm min.

600mm min. (400mm min. if trailer is less than 1300mm overall width)

The following are obligatory lamps required on all trailers:

There must be two red rear position lamps of the approved type.

Two red reflex reflectors of the approved type must be fitted (note that triangular reflectors may be fitted to trailers ONLY).

Where the towing vehicle is fitted with 'flashing' type indicators, the trailer must also be fitted with either one or two indicator lights on each side showing to the rear. These must operate in unison with the towing vehicle indicators, and the flashing frequency must be between 60 and 120 flashes per minute. It may be necessary to fit a heavy duty flasher unit to the towing vehicle in order to achieve that rate.

The rear number plate on a trailer is required to be adequately illuminated by an indirect light. This may be a separate light or may form part of the rear light cluster.

Trailers manufactured before 1 January 1971 must have at least one stop-lamp mounted either in the centre or to the offside of the rear, and all trailers manufactured after that date must have two stop lamps.

Stop lamps must show a red light which is non-flashing and of the approved type.

It is also obligatory for trailers first used on or after 1 April 1980 to have *at least one* rear fog lamp. If only one is fitted it must be positioned on or to the right of centre. When a trailer has two fog lamps they must be placed equidistant on either side of the centre of the trailer. They must show a steady non-flashing red light, and only be used in conditions where visibility is seriously reduced. It is an offence to wire fog lamps in such a way that they light up when the vehicle brakes are applied, and drivers must be able to see some sort of device which will indicate when the fog lights are on.

Trailers in excess of 1600mm in width must be fitted with front corner lights similar in size and design to the towing vehicle's front side lamps. Trailers manufactured before 1 October 1985 with an overall length (excluding any draw-bar and fitting attachment) not exceeding 2300mm are exempt from this requirement.

If reversing lights are fitted they must show a white light, and each lamp must be limited to a maximum of 24 watts. Unless the act of engaging reverse gear automatically lights up the reversing light there must also be a device to warn when the lights are switched on.

For trailers with an overall length of 5m or more (excluding any draw-bar) amber side reflex reflectors must be fitted. At least two must be fitted to each side of the trailer within specified positioning limits.

Trailers having a maximum gross weight of 3500kg must be fitted with a red and yellow fluorescent striped rear marking.

It is an offence to show a red light to the front of the vehicle, or a white light to the rear, except when reversing, unless it is illuminating the interior of the vehicle or trailer or the number plate. When reflex coated materials are used on number plates, the reflected light can be looked upon as 'showing a light'.

The lights and reflectors which are required by law must be maintained in clean, working order at all times. The fact that a vehicle or trailer is intended to be used only during the hours of daylight is not considered to be an acceptable excuse for failing to comply with the regulations.

Electrical System

Trailers derive their electrical power from the towing vehicle. Dirt and water can cause problems because the connection between the towing vehicle and the trailer is in a vulnerable position for catching any spray and dirt thrown up from the road. Similarly, most of the trailer lights are also at the rear of the vehicle where dirt and moisture are a hazard.

The following simple rules will help you to avoid electrical problems:

The connecting plugs should always be secured and kept dry when disconnected from the towing vehicle, and blanking flaps or dummy plugs are needed to protect the connecting points. Connecting plugs that are allowed to drop carelessly to the ground usually end up with cracked connectors, or dirty, wet connections.

Before connecting up, it is important to ensure that the male and female connectors are free of dirt or water, because even slight dampness can lead to a short circuit. Too much slack in the electrical leads between the towing vehicle and the trailer can also cause problems, particularly if the lead can come into contact with the ground, wearing away the insulation and ultimately causing a break in the circuit. The wiring on the trailer should be properly secured, well away from any moving parts that could trap or pinch the wires. Expert electricians should ensure that the circuiting is correct, and that all the joints are properly made.

Bulbs must be replaced with those of similar type and wattage. Fuses in the towing vehicle burn out when a fault develops in the circuit, and it is important to trace the fault before replacing the fuse, which again should always be of the same capacity as the one being replaced.

In order to achieve uniformity between all trailers and caravans, the connection between the towing vehicle and the trailer circuits has been standardised in the form of a seven-pin plug and socket. The plug can only be inserted in the socket in one position, and as the wiring-looms for towing vehicles and trailers have been colour-coded, individual circuits can be traced by the colour of the wire.

The standard colours are as follows:

Pin 1 **Nearside indicator** yellow
Pin 2 **Rear fog lamp** blue
Pin 3 **Earth** white
Pin 4 **Offside indicator** green
Pin 5 **Offside tail light** brown
Pin 6 **Stop lights** red
Pin 7 **Nearside tail and**
      number plate light black

The pins are normally numbred and set out as illustrated below:

Trailer wiring

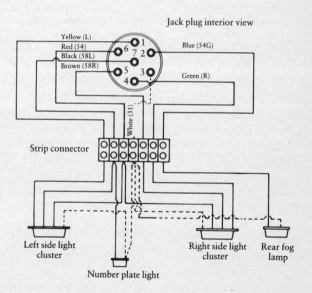

Different colours may be found on certain vehicles manufactured outside the United Kingdom and EEC countries, but a wiring circuit diagram and details of wire colours can generally be found in the manufacturer's handbook. Most vehicles are fitted with an earth return system in which the circuit back to the battery is completed by utilizing the chassis and the frame of the vehicle. Many minor electrical faults occur because of poor earth connections, either between the battery and frame or between a component and the

19

frame. In the case of trailers the number 3 pin connection must be satisfactory or the trailer lights will be affected.

If a single lamp fails to light, the bulb may be at fault, but if a new bulb does not solve the problem, it means that the bulb holder has become corroded or damp. It may then be necessary to dismantle the lamp holder and examine the mounting to make sure that there is a clean contact with an unpainted portion of the bodywork.

Other common electrical faults are: loose bulbs, wire insulation which has become chafed or cracked, blown fuses, loose fuses or faulty connections.

When the direction indicators are not functioning correctly the first sign of trouble is normally from the warning light on the dashboard which may not flash or light up at all unless all the indicators are working. If an exterior check shows that all the indicators *are* working, the problem with the warning light may indicate a defect in the bulb, its holder, or even the flasher unit. Some vehicles are wired in such a way that the warning light will continue to function even though one indicator light is defective, but in such cases it is possible that the rate of flashing at the warning lamp will be affected and thus warn the driver.

The failure of indicators to flash at the correct rate of between 60 and 120 times a minute may be due to bulbs being fitted which are defective or of incorrect wattage, lack of a heavy duty flasher unit or to poor connections in the circuit or fuses.

All electrical circuits and connections should be kept clean, tightly secured and dry. Many problems with trailers are caused by neglect; because of their simplicity of design, and perhaps their somewhat infrequent usage, there is a tendency for owners not to give them the attention that they warrant. This can lead to accidents and to costly repair bills. Wise owners get to know their trailers and study the manufacturer's advice in the handbook.

Chapter 2

Repairs and Maintenance of Trailers

Unlike a towing vehicle a trailer has few major mechanical components that are likely to give trouble. The main problems usually occur in the electrical system (which has already been described) or the braking system, the suspension, and the road wheels.

The Braking System

The majority of horse trailers are equipped with over-run brakes. These are activated when the towing vehicle slows down and the trailer attempts to over-run the towing vehicle. Pressure is exerted through the coupling, and this is transferred to a linkage which applies the brakes on the trailer wheels. On some trailers the pressure on the coupling has to overcome the tension of a large spring before activating the trailer brake linkage. This spring is necessary in order to avoid application of the trailer brakes in normal driving through the constant movement between the two vehicles.

It also follows that in first having to overcome the tension of this spring when braking, there will be a slight delay before the trailer brakes are applied. With this type of braking system the driver therefore needs to be particularly careful, or the occupants of the trailer will have a rather uncomfortable ride.

The spring type of trailer brake is now being replaced by a system wherein the pressure at the coupling is transmitted to the trailer brake linkage through a hydraulically controlled piston. This system provides a much more progressive braking action at the trailer wheels whilst still preventing undue brake application in normal driving.

Apart from cleaning and lubricating, little attention is required by either type of system, but if a major defect occurs in either the spring or the hydraulic system, repairs should be carried out by the manufacturer or his accredited agent.

The systems so far described are concerned only with the conversion of the pressure at the coupling into initial activation of the trailer brake system. As to the trailer brake system itself, the type usually found on all but the heaviest of trailers consists of a linkage of rods or cables terminating at the brake drums to which the road wheels are attached. The linkage incorporates a compensating device which ensures that an equal amount of pressure is exerted at each wheel being braked.

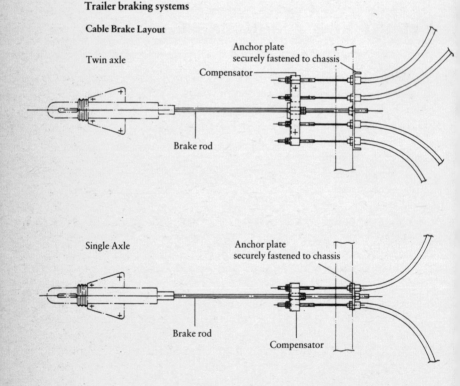

Trailer braking systems

Cable Brake Layout

Twin axle

Anchor plate securely fastened to chassis

Compensator

Brake rod

Single Axle

Anchor plate securely fastened to chassis

Brake rod

Compensator

Rod Brake Layout

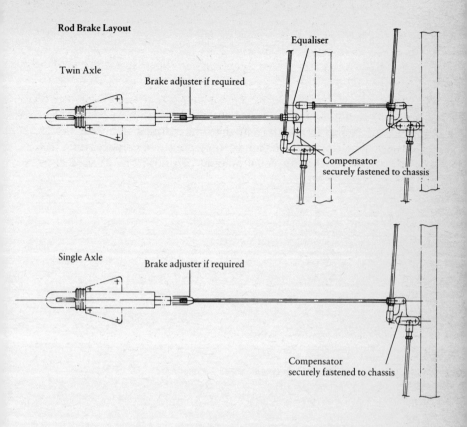

So that the system will function correctly it is necessary for the cables or rods to move without impediment, and for each joint or coupling in the linkage also to have free movement. A linkage caked in mud or rusted to the point of seizure will have a seriously adverse effect on the efficiency of the brakes – to a point where, in extreme circumstances, they will not function at all.

The linkage also has a means of adjusting the tension, because when the brakes are off it is important that there is a little slack to ensure a complete withdrawal of pressure at the brake drum. The manufacturer's handbook will give guidance as to the correct method of trailer brake linkage adjustment.

Even with a correctly adjusted linkage, however, there is still a possibility of brake malfunction on the trailer. A defect may be only of a temporary nature, for instance if the wheels on one side of the trailer went through a large puddle and water got into the drums on one side. Normal braking would soon dissipate the water and the braking efficiency would quickly return. If oil or grease from the wheel hub finds its way on to the brake shoes, the same one-sided braking effect will be noticed. When this happens it will normally be necessary to strip down the brake drum and shoes in order to clean off the oil or grease.

A more common cause of uneven braking is uneven adjustment of the brake shoes. There is usually a way of adjusting brake shoes on the back of each brake plate. The trailer wheel should be jacked up clear of the ground with the remaining wheels securely chocked and the brakes fully released. The adjuster can then be turned until the brake is fully applied and the wheel cannot be turned. The adjuster should then be slowly reversed until the wheel can be revolved and the brake shoes are just clear of the drum.

All the braked wheels should be adjusted in this way and the trailer should be towed along a straight, level and hard surface for the brake application to be finally tested.

Adjusting the brakes of a trailer

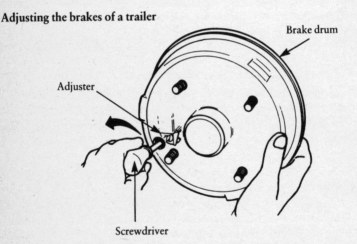

The Suspension System
    The majority of horse trailers now incorporate independent suspension systems of the torsion bar type. These systems are admirable in that they have the minimum of moving parts, require little or no servicing, and provide the best possible ride for the trailer's occupants.

The older, leaf spring system, still to be found on some trailers, can suffer from broken spring leaves, loose spring hanger brackets, and wear in the shackle and pivot pins. There is also the inconvenience of having to lubricate the pivot pins when they are fitted in metal bushes.

Whatever the type of suspension, a trailer when unladen and parked on level ground should sit squarely in relation to the ground. Any lean to one side may denote a weakness in the suspension on that side. For confirmation, the gap between the top of the road wheels and the underside of the body should be compared, and if a weakness is noticeable a skilled mechanic should be called.

In the case of leaf springs the angle at which the spring shackles are lying should be examined for signs of general weakness in the spring. The sides of the spring leaves should be cleaned with a wire brush and the main leaf examined for any signs of cracks or breaks. The main leaf is the only part of the spring which is directly connected to both the chassis and the axle, and a broken main leaf could result in the axle becoming detached from the trailer.

General Maintenance

Trailers in constant use require frequent maintenance checks and all should be given at least periodic attention.

Manufacturers normally provide advice on maintenance, but the following general advice should be followed whenever possible:

Before a trailer is used the interior should be cleaned and examined for any signs of deterioration in the body or the floor. A floor rotted by urine from a horse or pony can be very dangerous.

Tyres should be examined for cuts or signs of wear or damage which would make them illegal, and the pressures should be checked.

The exterior of the trailer should be examined for any dangerous projections or possible damage.

The coupling and braking equipment should be examined and lubricated where necessary.

After the trailer has been coupled up to the towing vehicle the lights and indicators should be examined to make sure that they are working properly. Also check that the lamp lenses, reflectors and number plates are clean.

Immediately after a trailer has been used the wheel hubs should be checked for any sign of heat. Excessive heat could indicate a defective hub bearing and the need for a major service.

If a trailer has to be left unused for some time the following action is needed:

The trailer should be cleaned thoroughly inside and out, and the usual daily check carried out. It should then be sited on firm level ground. If jacks are fitted they should be lowered fully, and if the ground is soft or uneven, wooden or metal blocks should be used.

The jockey wheel should be lowered, and, by using the adjusting handle on the top, the front of the trailer should be raised slightly so that its weight is supported by a combination of the jockey wheel, the corner jacks, and the normal suspension and road wheels.

The exterior electrical wiring and the connecting plug should be cleaned. The wiring and plug should be examined for any signs of damage or deterioration, and any fault should be rectified. The connecting plug and the loose cable in the vicinity of the coupling housing should be secured, and both should be covered with a plastic bag or some other waterproof material. If you use a plastic bag, do not tie it tightly round the plug and cable or condensation will form inside the bag.

If the trailer is left parked for long periods, the road wheels should be revolved from time to time in order to relieve the pressure on any one part of the tyre.

Although a separate Ministry of Transport Certificate is not needed for horse trailers, they are required to be maintained in a thoroughly roadworthy condition, and all the equipment must be in working order. There should also be nothing loose or broken on the body which could cause danger to other road users.

Chapter 3

The Towing Vehicle and the Driver

The Towing Vehicle

The advice given by the Caravan Club to its members is also valid for people buying horse trailers: 'Select the largest, most powerful car you can afford, and the smallest trailer that will adequately satisfy your needs'.

If that advice is followed the best power-to-weight ratio will be achieved. Most manufacturers provide the necessary information for vehicles used in towing trailers. This will include the kerb-weight, the maximum recommended towing weight, and the recommended nose-weight of any trailer.

The major factors affecting the recommended maximum towing weight are the kerb-weight and the engine power available. The nose-weight is the force which is exerted by the trailer on to the towing attachment at the rear of the towing vehicle. Horse trailers are so designed that when fully loaded the nose-weight is well within the acceptable limits for the vehicles generally used for towing.

Couplings

There are two types of coupling used for securing trailers. The first and most common in use on horse trailers is the towing-ball-and-socket connection. In the United Kingdom the metal ball mounted on a frame at the rear of the towing vehicle has a standard diameter of 50mm. Some old trailers are still fitted with a 2-in (50.8-mm) ball, and it should be noted that an adequate, safe connection cannot be made between the old 2-in ball and the modern 50-mm socket.

The other type of connection is usually found on the heavier goods trailer. It consists of a metal eye at the end of the trailer tow-bar which locates in a bracket at the rear of the towing vehicle, and is retained in position by a metal pin which passes through both the bracket and the metal eye.

The design of modern vehicles almost universally necessitates the mounting of the tow-ball on a plate which is secured to the vehicle by a bracket or another plate. There are many proprietary brands of towing bracket kits specially designed to fit individual makes and models of towing vehicles. It is very important that the correct fitting is secured by someone who is an expert on the subject.

The towing balls are normally mounted about 18in from the ground, but the normal attitude of the trailer towing attachment may dictate a difference in ball height.

The towing ball needs to be greased before the trailer is coupled up, and it should have some sort of covering when not in use, to protect it from dirt. The seven-pin electrical socket which is also normally mounted on the tow-ball plate incorporates a spring-loaded cap. The cap should be kept closed when the trailer is not coupled.

Stabilizers

A variety of stabilizer units is now available. They are usually mounted on the tow-ball bracket assembly at the rear of the towing vehicle, and are connected by way of a loose connection to the tow-bar of the trailer. They permit the normal articulation of the driving vehicle and trailer when turning or cornering, but provide a resistance to 'snaking' or 'weaving about' by the trailer in normal straightforward driving conditions. This type of movement is more prevalent in single-axle, two-wheel trailers, than in two-axle, four-wheel, close-coupled trailers.

Towing experience will indicate whether an outfit would benefit from stabilizers being fitted, and trailer manufacturers will give advice on the best types.

Suspension Assisters

The rear suspension of an older towing vehicle may have been weakened, in which case a suspension assister can be fitted which will supplement the normal suspension. Trailer manufacturers will again advise on the fitting of such equipment.

Battery and Lights

The additional lighting required on the trailer will impose a heavier than usual load on the battery of the towing vehicle, and on the alternator, if one is fitted. It is therefore important that the battery be kept topped up with distilled water, and that terminal connections be kept tight, clear of corrosion, and protected with Vaseline or some other appropriate grease. The battery earth should also be in good condition and properly secured to the earthing point on the frame. When alternators are used, the tension of the fan belt can be critical, because even a slightly slack fan belt can cause reduced output and a flat battery.

A heavy-duty flasher unit is sometimes needed in order to maintain the correct rate of flashing when extra lamps are brought into the circuit. The same problem may occur with the brake-light circuit. If the stop lights are seriously under-illuminated when the brakes are applied a heavy duty mechanical relay switch will be required.

Plating and Testing

Dual purpose vehicles, and trailers equipped only with a hand-brake and over-run type brakes, are exempt from the requirement to be plated and tested under the Goods Vehicles (Plating and Testing) Regulations 1971, and the amending regulations which have come into effect since that date.

Tachographs

A later chapter deals with tachographs, but it is important to know that all goods-carrying vehicles which have a gross weight in excess of 3.5 tonnes must be fitted with a tachograph. The gross weight limit includes the maximum gross weight of any towing vehicle. Although most towing vehicles and trailers will have a gross vehicle weight of less than 3.5 tonnes, drivers of heavier dual-purpose vehicles (such as a Range Rover) towing larger horse trailers may exceed the limit.

Following representations made by the British Horse Society, the Department of Transport issued a press notice on 29 June 1981 expressing the view that equestrian leisure pursuits were likely to be regarded in law as 'cultural events', thus exempting horse trailer combinations exceeding 3.5 tonnes gross weight from the need for a tachograph. This relaxation in the law applies only to the PRIVATE use of horse transporting vehicles, and is limited to the United Kingdom.

Speed Limits

The speed limit can be determined by the road on which you are travelling or by the type of vehicle you are driving. When limits differ, the lower limit will always apply.

There is a national limit of 70mph on dual carriageways, and

60mph on single carriageways, unless a lower speed limit is indicated by the appropriate traffic sign. Restricted roads are those having a system of street lighting with lamps not more than 200 yards apart. On such roads the speed limit for all traffic is 30mph.

Vehicles towing trailers have further speed restrictions imposed upon them. On all other (i.e. not 'restricted') roads, including motorways, a speed limit of 50mph applies to cars, dual-purpose vehicles and car-derived vans which are towing one trailer, providing of course that no lower limit has been applied to the particular stretch of road.

Licences

Anyone driving a mechanically propelled vehicle on a public highway is required to hold a licence covering the type of vehicle being driven. A standard provisional licence permits the holder to drive a vehicle whilst under supervision and subject to certain other restrictions, but provisional licence holders are *not* allowed to drive vehicles towing a trailer.

Anyone 17 years of age or over holding a Group A licence may drive a vehicle up to 3.5 tonnes gross weight. The weight limit refers to the vehicle and its maximum permitted load weight, and also that of any trailer. At the age of 18 the weight restriction is automatically increased to 7.5 tonnes without any need to exchange or amend the Group A licence issued at 17.

With certain goods-vehicle operations it is necessary for the owner or operator to hold an Operator's Licence. But the majority of horse trailers are towed by cars or dual-purpose vehicles and would be exempt because their gross vehicle weight would be below 3.5 tonnes. If, however, the towing vehicle is rather large and the trailer is equipped to carry two or more large horses, owners would be wise to check on the maximum gross weight and to study the Goods Vehicles (Ascertainment of Maximum Gross Weights) Regulations 1976 (S.1 1976 No 555).

Drivers' Hours

As with goods vehicles, all vehicles towing goods-carrying trailers are bound by regulations governing the drivers' 'activities and operations'. For safety reasons these regulations limit the time which may be spent at the wheel, or otherwise working, and stipulate the time to be allowed for breaks for refreshment and rest.

There are three major systems of drivers' hours regulations — National, International and Domestic:

National regulations apply to the drivers and other crew members of vehicles which, including any trailer, have a gross weight in excess of 3.5 tonnes and are used within the United Kingdom. These regulations are a combination of EEC Regulation 543/69 and the Transport Act 1968.

International regulations again apply to vehicles with a gross weight in excess of 3.5 tonnes, but when used abroad on journeys to EEC member states. (Journeys to EEC non-member states are subject to a quite separate set of rules known as AETR regulations.) International regulations will apply to those parts of an international journey which take place to or from the port in the United Kingdom.

Domestic regulations apply to goods vehicles with a gross weight not exceeding 3.5 tonnes whose use is confined to the United Kingdom. Domestic regulations are derived from the Transport Act 1968 and differ markedly from the EEC-based National and International regulations, in that the driving of goods vehicles in a private capacity is entirely exempted from the scope of the regulations.

The regulations are complicated, containing as they do so many extensions and exemptions. Detailed guidance may be obtained at any Heavy Goods Vehicle Training Centre, the local office of the Road Transport Industry Training Board, or from the local Traffic Area Office.

Drivers' Records

In the majority of cases where regulations govern drivers' hours there is a requirement for the driver to maintain records of work, including the hours the vehicle is driven. Since 1 January 1982, these records have had to be recorded on a tachograph. There are, however, some exemptions, which include vehicles or vehicle and trailer combinations with a gross vehicle weight of no more than 3.5 tonnes, as well as specialized vehicles on national journeys, used only for cultural events, or used as mobile exhibitions.

Chapter 4

Hitching, Unhitching, Loading and Unloading

Hitching

Before dealing with driving techniques it is important that the basic principles of hitching and unhitching are clearly understood, otherwise both can become hard work, particularly if the driver is alone.

The procedure for hitching is as follows:

Check that the trailer's parking brake is applied and that the electrical leads and connectors are tucked away and not left in a vulnerable position.

Reverse the towing vehicle so that the towing ball is alongside the hitch on the trailer tow-bar. The help of a second person can be invaluable at this stage, but if help is not available the driver should be careful to stop short of the trailer if unsure of the exact whereabouts of the tow-bar.

Raise the level of the trailer draw-bar by means of the jockey wheel until the hitch is slightly higher than the top of the ball.

Manoeuvre the trailer until the hitch is above the ball. Moving the trailer on unmade ground can be simplified by using a block or a chock. Place the chock to the rear of one wheel, pull the draw-bar across in the direction of the chocked wheel, then apply the parking brake. Remove the chock and place it behind the wheel on the other side of the trailer. Release the parking brake and pull the draw-bar across in the opposite direction (i.e. towards the chocked wheel). In this way the trailer can be manoeuvred into the desired position with the minimum of physical effort.

When the hitch is positioned directly over the ball, check that the security lock is released, then lower the hitch on to the ball by winding down the jockey wheel. An audible click can be heard when the coupling is made and secured by the locking device.

Wind the jockey wheel up fully and secure it in the travelling position. Check that the connection has been made properly by pulling upwards on the trailer draw-bar.

Examine the electrical components for cleanliness and ensure that they are dry. When satisfied, make the connection.

Start the vehicle engine. Switch on all the lights and check that they are working properly on the vehicle and the trailer. Remember to check the brake lights and indicators.

Release the trailer parking brake and make sure that the clip on the tow-bar has not been left in the reversing position.

If stabilizers are fitted, connect them and attach the breakaway cable.

Adjust the wing mirrors to take into account the width of the trailer and the height of the driver.

Prepare the trailer for loading.

Loading

Before the horse trailer is loaded, the driver should make sure that it is hitched securely to the driving vehicle and that as far as possible it is on firm, level ground. The interior should also be clean and free of any defects which could cause injury to the horse. Any loose tack, buckets or other equipment should be removed. The corner jacks or stays should be lowered before putting down the loading ramp.

There is a range of protective equipment designed to prevent injury to horses during transit, and investment in such equipment is never wasted.

Having prepared both the trailer and the horse, the loading process should take place without fuss. Horses being transported for the first time usually benefit by having an older or more experienced animal loaded first. Once the horse is in the trailer, the headcollar should be secured with enough slack on the rope or chain to allow the horse to have head movement. The partitions must be secured firmly, and when only one horse is being carried in a two-horse trailer it is best to place the horse on the off-side so that its weight will counter-balance the effect of the road camber. The opposite is true on the Continent.

Hay nets should be away from the animal's eyes and high enough to ensure that when empty they cannot get tangled with the horse's feet.

Finally, close and secure the loading ramp and door and raise the corner jacks and stays fully. Then check the ventilation to ensure that there is a constant supply of fresh air.

During the Journey

On long journeys, regular stops should be made to see that the occupants of the trailer are all right. Regulations governing the transit of horses require that an adequate supply of food and water should be available at intervals of not more than 12 hours.

Unloading

At the conclusion of a journey, before unloading it is important to ensure that the trailer is on firm and level ground, that the corner jacks or stays are lowered and secured, and that when the loading ramp is lowered the whole of the leading edge is in firm contact with the ground.

Regulations demand that if the unloading process completes the work for the day, any straw must be removed and the trailer cleaned and disinfected.

Unhitching

The procedure for unhitching is basically the hitching system in reverse, namely:

Apply the parking brake. If the trailer is on a gradient, chock the wheels on both sides.

Disconnect any stabilizers and the breakaway cable.

Disconnect the electrical connection and secure the lead on the draw-bar. Ensure that the dust caps on the electrical plugs are in position.

Lower the jockey wheel until it is just in contact with the ground. If there are horses on board, they should now be unloaded.

Release the hitch lock and raise the level of the tow-bar by means of the jockey wheel until the hitch is clear of the ball.

Drive the vehicle clear of the trailer.

If the trailer is to be left for some time, lower the corner jacks or stays until the weight of the trailer with the animals removed is supported on a combination of jacks, road wheels and the jockey wheel.

Cover the towing ball to protect it against mud, grit and weather.

Chapter 5

Techniques of Driving with Trailers

Basic Driving Techniques

Different driving techniques are required when towing a trailer, and although there are no courses for people wishing to tow a horse trailer, the Caravan Club provides courses for people new to caravanning, which can be very useful. Membership of the Club is not necessary; the address is East Grinstead House, East Grinstead, West Sussex RH19 1UA.

Many drivers new to towing trailers show a tendency to use too high engine revolutions while slipping the clutch when moving off. This can lead to excessive clutch wear. The answer is to use just enough engine power to allow the clutch to be engaged fully and then to increase the power and gently accelerate away. Avoid harsh acceleration, and when moving away in traffic remember that a vehicle towing a trailer will move more slowly and will need a larger than normal gap in the traffic.

When moving away, imagine that you are standing up in a bus. Horses are much larger and heavier and will tend to sway about more than a human passenger.

Changing gear should be done smoothly, again avoiding a tendency to over-rev and slip the clutch.

When the time comes to slow down, and perhaps stop, it should be remembered that the combined weight of the towing vehicle and the trailer, together with the weight and characteristics of a live load, will call for a very different driving technique from that required in a standard vehicle without a trailer. Harsh or emergency breaking should be avoided as far as possible, or the load will be thrown forward.

The driver should always look as far ahead as possible and try and anticipate problems which may necessitate braking or stopping. The sooner that trouble is spotted the sooner the driver can do something about it. If it is only possible to see a short distance ahead, then the road speed should be kept down so that even in the limited distance available a progressive and normal stop can be made if a problem arises.

When bringing the vehicle and trailer to a halt, the driver should try to avoid maintaining pressure on the brake pedal, which may cause the vehicle to jolt. The pressure should be released slightly just before coming to a standstill, thus easing the vehicle and trailer to a stop. If the driver can imagine motoring with a full glass of water on the bonnet, then the right attitude to braking and accelerating will be achieved.

With the speed limits in force for trailer-towing vehicles it is inevitable that they will be overtaken more frequently than they will overtake. Care is necessary in both circumstances.

Good exterior mirrors are essential on every towing vehicle, and particular attention should be paid to them to ensure that the driver is always fully aware of the traffic situation behind him. When someone prepares to overtake you, you should take special note of the road ahead in case the overtaking vehicle has to pull in sharply, either because of poor judgement of distance and speed, or because he or she misjudged the length of the vehicle and trailer. The driver of the towing vehicle must follow the advice of the Highway Code and never accelerate when being overtaken, and must avoid having to brake sharply.

Passing Stationary Vehicles

When passing a stationary vehicle the following procedure is the safest:

The driver should look well ahead of the hazard and make sure that the manoeuvre can be completed safely at normal speed.

If oncoming traffic makes passing a risk, the driver must slow down and if necessary stop well back from the obstruction.

The right indicator should be left on to dissuade following traffic from overtaking and complicating the situation.

There must always be a reasonable distance between the towing vehicle and the obstruction to be passed.

When the road is clear the driver should check in his mirrors and pull out gently, passing the obstruction on a parallel path before returning to the near side of the road as soon as it is practical and safe, paying particular attention to the nearside mirror.

Overtaking

When overtaking moving vehicles it is important to remember that the speed differential may be quite small, and the vehicle to be passed may be up to 50ft (50.38m) in length in the case of a standard articulated goods vehicle.

The following procedure should be adopted:

From a position well to the rear of the vehicle to be overtaken the driver should assess the speed of the vehicle and the distance needed to overtake safely in view of the road and weather conditions, and the speed, acceleration, length and load of the driver's own vehicle and trailer.

Once the driver is satisfied that the conditions are right, that traffic is not emerging from any side roads, and that he is not approaching a steep hill or a bend which may alter his ability to overtake safely, he should look in his mirrors and clearly signal his intentions before pulling out.

It should be remembered that there is a considerable amount of air turbulence involved when overtaking large, slab-sided vehicles, and it is important for both drivers to be aware of the situation. The steering wheel should be held firmly, and careful use should be made of the mirrors.

The main rule for a driver to remember is, 'when in doubt, hold back'.

General

As a horse's or a pony's volume may be considered to be 'top weight', allowance must always be made for undulations in the road surface, bends, cambers, corners and roundabouts, and there must never be any sharp movements which could throw the horse off his feet, or cause him to swing about in his stall.

The nearside is normally the bumpiest part of the road, and the towing vehicle and trailer should not be driven too close to the edge except when necessary. On poorly maintained roads the tarmac·may also be broken at the edge and the driver should be on the look-out for any sign of 'tramlining' (where heavy traffic has worn ruts in the road). If the trailer is wider than the towing vehicle, allowance must be made for this fact when negotiating potholes and bumps.

The suspension of the towing vehicle will probably absorb most bumps, but the same is not always the case with the suspension of the trailer, and the horses or ponies inside can often be subjected to a very rough ride without the driver being aware of it. One has only to see trailers being driven over rough ground at a show to realise this fact. Horses can soon learn to adapt to various road conditions providing they are not subjected to any sudden movement, and that, whenever possible, accelerating and braking is carried out slowly and gradually.

Bends and Corners

Particular care is necessary when deviating from a straight line, because when that happens other forces will be exerted on the vehicle. Centrifugal force will tend to push the vehicle and its trailer back on to a straight path, which in certain circumstances can result in a skid. The sharper the deviation, the slower your speed should be.

Bends should always be taken carefully, and if they are arrowed the chances are that the curves will be significant. A driver should watch his speed and follow the course of the bend, braking as little as possible and using a light touch on the accelerator. When the view and road ahead are clear he can accelerate away from the bend and again build up speed. Heavy braking and harsh acceleration should be avoided.

Problems encountered when turning with a trailer

Kerbing

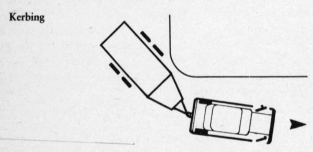

The trailer effectively lengthens the total wheelbase, and consequently it is necessary to compensate by a slight widening of the turning circle to avoid 'kerbing'.

Turning corners with a trailer also requires a slightly different technique. When turning into a junction on the left it will be necessary on approach to move further out from the kerb than usual, in order to allow for the additional length of the vehicle, and a certain degree of 'cut-in' by the trailer. The correct position for the approach should be adopted early, and intentions should be signalled in good time. Again the sharper the turn, the lower the speed will need to be. The nearside mirror will be most important for showing whether any cyclists or motor cyclists are approaching on the inside. This is particularly true at road junctions which may be controlled by traffic lights and whenever vehicles have had to stop before turning to the left.

Clipping

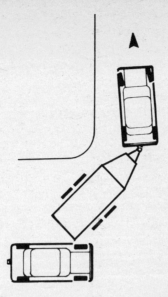

With a trailer that has a fairly long overhang, there is a danger that if the sweep is completed too sharply, the tail will swing round and collide with another vehicle.

Turning to the right is a particularly dangerous manoeuvre because it involves crossing the path of oncoming traffic. It is necessary to pay particular attention to the mirrors and to signal one's intentions well in advance. The correct position on approach will depend to a certain extent on the width of the road. If the road is wide enough, the driver should pull over towards the crown of the road to allow following traffic to pass by on the left. Speed should be reduced gently and the correct gear selected. It may be necessary to stop and wait for a suitable opportunity to turn, bearing in mind the length of and speed restriction imposed by the trailer. If the road is clear of oncoming traffic, however, and if there is no one trying to overtake, the turn can be made, taking into account any traffic on the side road. If it is necessary to wait, the towing vehicle should be brought to a halt opposite the entrance to the side road, with the vehicle and trailer parallel to the crown of the road.

When it is safe to proceed, the driver must be careful not to cut the corner or to interfere with any traffic on the side road. Harsh acceleration should be avoided. If the side road is narrow, and there are vehicles waiting to exit on to the main road, it may be necessary to stop slightly short of the normal position, and wait for the junction to clear before turning. A little patience may prevent the entrance from becoming blocked.

Roundabouts

Roundabouts should be treated according to their position and size. The Highway Code gives clear advice as to the correct positioning on approach, the best method of negotiating the roundabout, and the correct method of exit. The following basic rules should be obeyed:

If you are turning left or going straight on, approach on the left.

Only approach on the right if you are going straight on or turning right.

Signal left on approach only if you are turning left at the first exit from the roundabout.

Signal right on approach only if you are turning right and leaving by an exit after the one leading straight ahead.

Signal left when you pass the exit before the one you intend to leave by.

Give way to traffic which is already on the roundabout.

Special care must be taken on roundabouts by drivers of vehicles towing trailers, not only because of the speed and length of the combination, but because rearward vision may be impeded by the vehicle and trailer moving out of alignment when turning. Small roundabouts should be taken in the same way as larger ones but it is wise to watch out for other drivers who go straight over the small round bumps in the centre. Multiple mini-roundabouts are not easy to negotiate, but the same advice applies.

Chapter 6

Problems with Towing Trailers

It has already been emphasised that the ability to tow a trailer containing horses or ponies requires a hundred percent concentration, and a very responsible approach to the condition and performance of the towing vehicle and trailer. Problems, however, can still occur and drivers should be aware of how best to deal with them.

Pitching

A common problem is known as 'pitching'. Even in normal driving on a good surface an oscillating motion fore and aft may be experienced, and there are a number of possible causes. When a trailer is unhitched and standing on its own it is normal for there to be a slight downward pressure on the hitch end of the draw-bar. This nose-weight is counteracted in normal driving by the air passing beneath the trailer and lifting the front, thus maintaining an overall position level with the driving vehicle. An excess of nose-weight, however, can lead to the outfit pitching when travelling. Some horses tend to sit back when travelling, and this can also tend to upset the balance.

Trailer manufacturers will advise on the acceptable nose-weight and this can be measured by means of a gauge placed beneath the hitch and the ground.

If the trailer nose-weight is within acceptable limits, the pitching may be caused by the tow-ball being sited at the wrong height on the towing vehicle, or by a weakness in the suspension of the towing vehicle. In the case of suspension weakness a suspension assister may cure the problem.

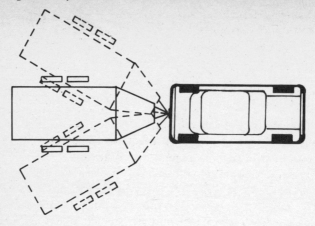

Snaking

The problem of 'snaking', when the trailer sways from side to side, is attributed to excessive towing speed and usually occurs on motorways. It can be aggravated by combinations of incorrect weight distribution on the trailer, wrong tyre pressures, cross-wind gusts and buffet from heavy vehicles when overtaking. The correct response to snaking is to remain calm and steadily to reduce speed until the oscillation stops of its own accord. Attempts to hasten the process by braking will merely intensify the snaking.

Snaking

Another problem is known as 'snaking'. In normal driving the trailer begins to sway from side to side, and when this occurs there are some definite 'dos' and 'don'ts' for the driver:

He should take his foot off the accelerator and allow the vehicle to decelerate on its own until the snaking stops.

He should allow the steering wheel to twitch slightly in his hands and at the same time try to maintain a straight or slightly curved path.

He should *not* accelerate in an attempt to pull the vehicle and trailer straight.

He should *not* brake as this may cause the trailer to jack-knife or even overturn.

He should *not* attempt to counteract the snaking by steering left and right. By doing so he will probably get it wrong and exacerbate the situation.

If snaking develops when travelling downhill the brakes may be used very gently to control the speed but only a light pressure should be used.

Snaking can be induced by wind or when passing large slab-sided vehicles, but if the snaking occurs frequently the tyre pressures should be checked and the suspension system should also be tested for any signs of weakness. A special stabilizer fitted between the towing vehicle and the trailer can help to prevent snaking.

Mirrors and Obstructions

When problems occur it is vital for the driver to have the assistance of good quality large mirrors fitted externally on both sides of the towing vehicle, so that he can be fully aware of the traffic situation to the side and behind him, as well as in front. It is also important to know the height of the trailer. Although horse trailers will pass safely below most bridges, there are other hazards such as overhanging trees, shop blinds, and road signs. A steep camber on the road may also tilt the trailer over to a point when the roof may strike obstructions, with obvious danger to the horses.

The fuel consumption of the towing vehicle is bound to be increased by the weight and shape of the trailer, and it will often be necessary to refuel during a journey. Canopies and signs at filling stations can present a problem, and special care should be taken when approaching the fuel pumps.

Winds

Horse trailers are susceptible to cross-winds as well as turbulence caused by large vehicles either overtaking or being overtaken. Experienced drivers anticipate problems and take note of the various road and weather signs which can spell trouble. Swaying trees and bushes can indicate the presence of strong winds. Gaps in hedges and walls, or between bridges or banking on motorways can all be danger spots because winds can be funnelled through at increased velocity. A vehicle ahead which suddenly veers off-line for no apparent reason can signify the presence of a cross-wind.

Stops

Frequent stops on long journeys not only give the driver an opportunity to relax for a few minutes, they also give the horses a rest from the constant movement. A lay-by is the best place to stop, and the driver will have room to do a quick check of the driving vehicle, the trailer and its load in comparative safety without inconveniencing other road users.

The following should be checked:

Tyres A visual check can be useful, as pressures can vary on a journey due to frictional heat, and a tyre gauge can thus give a misleading reading.

Hubs Feel the wheel hubs for any signs of excessive heat which can indicate dry bearings or binding brakes.

Lights Lamp lenses should be cleaned, because dirt will affect performance. If dusk is approaching, it is as well to check that everything is in order.

Coolant and Oil During stops of longer than 20 minutes it is always wise to check the radiator level, and the level of the engine oil. Make sure that the radiator is cooled sufficiently before opening the cap.

Fan belt While the bonnet is open, check the fan belt for any signs of slackness which will affect the lights. A spare fan belt should always be carried on long journeys.

The Horses Always check the trailer's occupants and see whether they need food and water. Check ventilation and see whether rugs and bandages need adjusting.

Hills

Climbing steep hills with a trailer can sometimes be a problem unless care is taken. Drivers should watch out for warning signs, and apart from increasing road speed to cater for the gradient, they should also change down through the gears in plenty of time so that a steady momentum can be maintained. Unless a stop is essential it is much easier to keep going in low gear than to stop and move off again on a steep gradient.

If the trailer has to be brought to a halt on a steep hill and it is difficult to hold the vehicles stationary, the steering wheel should be turned to the right so that if the trailer does run backwards it will be steered into the bank or hedge. It may be possible to move off again when the traffic permits. Two triangular blocks of wood to put behind the wheels of the trailer can be extremely useful, and if they are secured to the chassis by a loose length of rope they can be towed behind the trailer until it reaches the top of the hill, when the blocks can be returned to a safe place.

Low gear should be engaged when going down steep hills, and by making use of the brakes it should be a simple matter to choose the best gear before starting the descent.

Reversing

Reversing with a trailer can prove to be quite difficult and there are some basic rules which should be observed:

Reversing in a straight line is always easier than trying to manoeuvre the trailer at an angle, and the driver should try to begin by positioning the towing vehicle and trailer as far as possible in line with the entrance, or the position for the trailer to be parked.

If a straight reverse is not possible the unit should be reversed 'right hand down' so that the trailer's movement towards its objective can be watched out of the driver's door.

Reverse slowly, preferably at engine tick-over speed, because excess speed will make corrections more difficult.

Reversing round a corner

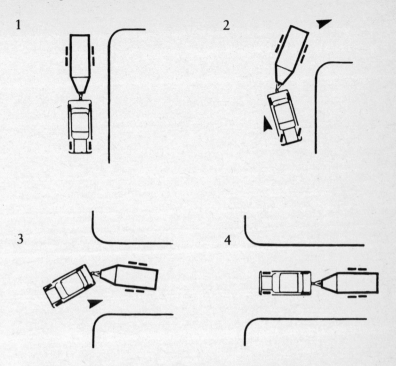

1 Commence with the trailer and the towing vehicle in a straight line.

2 Move slowly backwards, gradually applying opposite wheel lock to the direction of the turn.

3 When the trailer is moving on the right curve, transfer to normal steering lock and follow the trailer around the curve.

4 To complete the manoeuvre, straighten up towing vehicle and trailer.

If you lose control whilst reversing, stop, pull forward and start again. If you continue, you will jack-knife the trailer.

Only small steering corrections should be made. Over-correcting will result in the vehicles jack-knifing.

If the vehicle and trailer do jack-knife, the driver should stop, pull forward and start again. A complete jack-knife (when the trailer strikes the towing vehicle) can be expensive.

Before reversing it is essential to make sure that the reversing catch is in position, or the trailer will be reversed with the brakes applied.

Reversing round a corner requires a considerable amount of practice, but reversing in a straight line is relatively simple when carried out slowly, and if the driver watches the movement of the trailer in both exterior mirrors. If more of the trailer begins to appear in one mirror the steering wheel should be turned slightly in that direction. If it is not possible to use the mirrors, the driver should look out of his door and watch the right side of the trailer. If it goes off-line he should correct it by steering in the same direction. When the reversing manoeuvre has been completed, the reversing catch or clip should be removed, or the trailer brakes will not work when the unit is driven forwards.

Motorway Driving

Motorway driving can be hazardous in high winds and drivers must observe the speed limits for vehicle and trailer combinations. Only the nearside and centre lanes may be used when towing trailers; the outside overtaking lane may only be used if temporary road signs are in force due to an accident or road works, or on the instructions of a policeman in uniform. It is always wise to drive in the centre of the lane. If a large vehicle is about to overtake, the turbulence can be minimised by steering slightly to the left when the overtaking vehicle is almost in line, first making sure that there is plenty of room on the nearside.

In case of a breakdown the driver should pull in to the hard shoulder and use the emergency telephone system to summon help, making it clear that it is a trailer unit with horses on board.

Animals should never be unloaded on the hard shoulder because the traffic density and noise could unsettle them, and cause them to bolt, with all the obvious consequences.

Towing on Unmade Ground

If it becomes necessary to leave the road and tow the trailer across unmade ground there are some basic guidelines to be followed.

If the towing vehicle is equipped with four-wheel drive this should be engaged before going on to the unmade ground. It may be too late once traction has been lost. The driver should plan his route before starting off, particularly if the ground is soft or marshy. Following other vehicles' tracks can be a mistake because they may be so deep that the vehicle will 'belly down' on the centre section.

The correct gear to use would be the highest possible to maintain forward motion, but the engine revs should be kept down because spinning wheels will only cause deep ruts and will bring the vehicle to a stop.

Steep gradients should be avoided as far as possible, but if it is necessary to negotiate a hill the driver should always go straight up or down and never across, because this may mean loss of traction and cause the trailer to jack-knife.

The driver should always maintain a firmer than normal grip on the wheel with the thumbs on top and not curled round inside the wheel. A thumb held inside the wheel can easily be fractured if a roadwheel hits a pothole or hidden rock, and causes the steering wheel to spin.

Driving at Night

When driving at night the driver should always remember the effect that the weight of the trailer may have on the headlight beams. It is an offence to cause dazzle to oncoming drivers, quite apart from the fact that the beams will not be on the road at the places where they can be of most help. Even in a dipped position the beams may still dazzle other road users and will need to be adjusted.

General

Apart from the guidelines outlined in this book, driving a vehicle which is towing a trailer is very much a matter of concentration and good common sense. When approaching a hazard the driver should slow down and if necessary stop until the right action can be taken. It is also important to remember that horses in trailers cannot usually see what is coming. Cutting in close to hedges and branches may not do any damage to the trailer but it can cause the occupants to become frightened and create problems inside the trailer.

Trailer Check List

Remember: *A trailer has the same components as a car, except for an engine and a gearbox. Therefore, like a car, a trailer needs regular service and attention to the following if you and your horse or pony are to travel safely.*

TYRES

Are they cracked, cut or perished? Do they have sufficient tread? Are they legal? If in doubt consult a tyre depot. They will be pleased to carry out a safety check. Always check the recommended tyre pressure — this is vital. Trailer tyres get 'curbed' more often than car tyres and therefore are more likely to be damaged. Look for bulges; secure trailer with wheel chocks, jack up the trailer and use additional axle stands or equivalent as a safety measure against jack collapse. Remove the wheels, check inside and outside walls. Check that the top of the inside of the tyre is not rubbing on the inside of the mudguard. If there is a rubbing mark then either the wheel bearings need attention or the sub axles are bent or you are over-loading the trailer.

FLOOR

Always remove wet straw and manure at the end of each day's use. Do not leave a permanently wet layer of muck on the floor of the trailer. This is the most common cause of floors rotting, no matter how the floor is constructed. Even worse, you cannot see if the floor is deteriorating and needs attention and you do not find out that you have a problem until your horse's feet go through the floor. A clean dry floor will last longer and your horses will be safer. When not in use, park your trailer with the rear ramp tight against the side of a barn or building so that the rain cannot be driven in. This applies even if you have a rear curtain or double doors over the ramp.

Regularly sweep the floor, clean out drain holes and test the timber with a sharp knife, screwdriver or similar implement. If the blade goes in easily or if you are in any doubt, take the trailer to your nearest dealer. Many trailers have double floors and the same test should be done from the underside.

Trailer floors are made from special timbers of plywoods, which from the manufacturer's experience are particularly resistant to moisture and urine, or the floors have been specially treated. Do not replace damaged floors with ordinary plywood or boards. Trailers fitted with rubber matting: any damaged area should be replaced promptly, however small, and the underside should be checked, as above.

WHEEL BEARINGS

Remove bearing caps and check condition of bearings. Pack with grease, adjust bearing nut and fit new split pin. Refit bearing cap.

LIGHTS

Check 7-pin connector plug and socket. Check visible wiring for cuts, etc. Check all lights for correct operation. Replace faulty bulbs. Inspect lenses and reflectors.

HANDBRAKE

Check operation and ensure that the brakes are in fact applied. Lubricate pivots and linkages and adjust where required.

TOW BALL HEIGHT

Check with the trailer manufacturer that the ball on your towing vehicle is at the correct height for your trailer. Ball too high: front of car or front of trailer lifts. Ball too low: rear of car or rear of trailer lifts.

Rod operated brakes

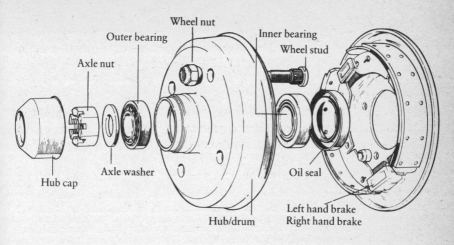

Wheel nut

Outer bearing

Inner bearing

Axle nut

Wheel stud

Hub cap

Axle washer

Oil seal

Hub/drum

Left hand brake
Right hand brake

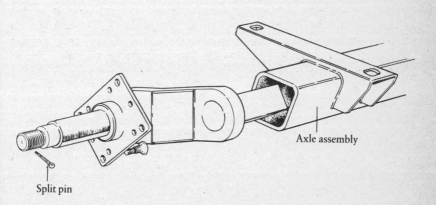

Axle assembly

Split pin

BRAKES

Remove brake drums, check linings, oil brake adjusters, clean out, dust with a damp cloth — do not remove dust with air pressure — re-fit drums. Free off, oil and grease brake pivots, actuating rods and compensators. Adjust brakes.

WARNING: Auto-reverse brakes are more sensitive than the older type of over-run brakes and they require more accurate adjustment. It is not recommended that the general public tries to adjust auto-reverse brakes.

BRAKE LINKAGE

Check all components for damage. Check tightness of all lock-nuts. Grease all moving parts.

The parts of a trailer coupling (delta type with ball coupling head)

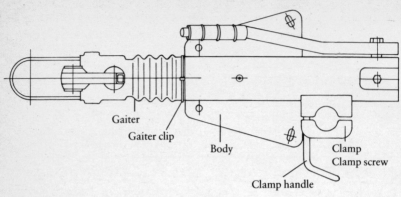

Gaiter

Gaiter clip

Body

Clamp
Clamp screw

Clamp handle

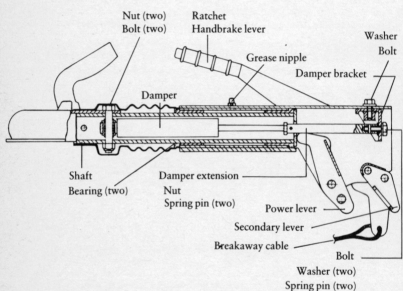

Nut (two)
Bolt (two)

Ratchet
Handbrake lever

Grease nipple

Washer
Bolt

Damper bracket

Damper

Shaft
Bearing (two)

Damper extension
Nut
Spring pin (two)

Power lever

Secondary lever

Breakaway cable

Bolt
Washer (two)
Spring pin (two)

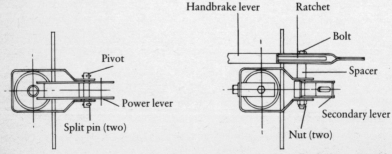

Pivot

Power lever

Split pin (two)

Power lever assembly

Handbrake lever

Ratchet

Bolt

Spacer

Secondary lever

Nut (two)

Secondary and handbrake lever assembly

COUPLING HEAD

Check locking handles and clips. Ensure that securing devices and locking springs function correctly. Check ball and coupling head for a loose fit. Both the ball and coupling wear and require lubrication. Check tightness of all nuts and bolts.

COUPLING BODY

Lubricate main shaft by applying grease to the drawtube by means of the grease nipple(s) on the coupling housing. Apply grease to the drawtube between the coupling head and coupling body. Check the dampers are functioning where fitted.

Chapter 7

Loading Horseboxes

Protective Clothing

Horses or ponies should never be transported in a trailer or a horsebox without protective clothing. Accidents can happen in spite of care being taken by the driver, and if a horsebox is in a collision, the occupants need all the protection they can get.

Starting with the head, a **headguard**, usually made of padded leather with ear holes, or a single strip of foam rubber, is often placed over the poll to give much needed protection for one of the most vulnerable parts of a horse. If a headguard is not available, and if the trailer or horsebox has a low roof, a bandage bound round the top of a headcollar and secured in place will give some protection.

Rugs help to protect a horse's sides when travelling, particularly when partitions do not have enough padding.

Stable bandages protect the legs and help to keep a horse warm in cold weather. They are usually made of woollen fabric or flannel about 8cm (3in) wide and 2.25m (7 or 8ft) in length. Two tapes are sewn at one end to hold the bandages in place on the horse's leg. Some owners save money by making their own stable bandages out of lengths of blanket. There are also some excellent proprietary brands of leg protectors now available.

To put a bandage on, it should first be neatly rolled, with the tapes folded in the middle, and then applied to the leg beginning just below the knee or hock. The bandage is wound downwards round the leg and fetlock joint as far as the coronet band, and is then wound upwards again. The tapes can be tied neatly below the knee with the knot on the outside of the cannon bone and never on the tendons.

Stable bandages should never be put on tightly but should be just firm enough to prevent them from slipping down. A layer of Gamgee tissue or foam rubber may be placed under the bandage to give additional warmth and protection during a journey.

Knee-caps and **hock-boots** are also valuable items of clothing for protecting vulnerable areas. The knee-cap consists of a strong, stiff leather pad, usually set in fabric. At the top there is a leather strap padded at the front which buckles fairly tightly above the knee and prevents the knee-cap from slipping downwards. The lower strap is buckled loosely below the knee in such a way that the joint can bend normally. The strap's function is really to stop the knee-cap from bending upwards.

The hock-boot is rather similar to the knee-cap and is also fixed at the top and bottom by leather straps. Its main purpose is to prevent injury to the hocks if the horse backs up hard against the rear of the trailer or horsebox.

A horse in transit will also require a thin and flexible **tail bandage**. This will prevent the top part of the tail from being rubbed and damaged when he leans against the back of the horsebox or the rear partition to get his balance. A tail bandage should not be applied too tightly, particularly if it is put on when the tail is damp.

A **tail-guard** may also be used. This is made of soft leather or thick woollen cloth. It is secured with tapes and an adjustable leather strap which runs from the top of the guard to the roller.

There are of course other items of protective clothing but these are the main essentials for safe travel.

Loading

Horses are usually a problem to load either because they are being asked to walk into something which they do not understand and cannot see into clearly, or because they have been transported badly on some previous occasion. This may have been due to inexperienced driving, or because the vehicle in which they were travelling was not suitable for their size, comfort or safety. Advice on loading trailers has been given in an earlier chapter, but loading into a horsebox can require a different technique.

Horseboxes are larger and are usually more stable than trailers, but they usually have steeper ramps because of the height of the chassis. For this reason they are more difficult for a horse to look into.

It is therefore important that the inside of a horsebox should be as light as possible, without dark corners and shadows to worry a nervous horse. Additional light can sometimes be thrown into a stall by opening access doors and making sure that any roof-lights are open. The partitions should be as wide open as possible and securely held in position so that they will not swing on to the horse when he starts to go up the ramp.

Ramps should always be secure. They should be covered with strong matting or ribbed rubber and have slats evenly placed to prevent a horse from slipping. The ramp opening should be as wide as possible and have adequate headroom.

A steep ramp is not always a handicap providing there is not a deep step at the top. Horses usually load better through side ramps. The reason is simple. A horse being taken up a rear ramp can more easily stop and run backwards, forcing his handler down the ramp after him. With a side ramp, however, as soon as the horse approaches the top of the ramp he is turned to start to go into his stall, whether it is on the off-side or the near-side of the horsebox. With his handler's shoulder against him preventing him from running sideways he can be urged to go forwards, and if he starts to run backwards he will more likely go into the back of the box, or the rear partition if he is being loaded into one of the forward stalls.

Young racehorses are usually loaded with the aid of a permanent loading ramp like a railway platform so that the horsebox's ramp is horizontal and level with the ground. A good solid bank will work the same way. Solid-type loading gates prevent the young horse from seeing either side of the ramp as he is encouraged to go forward, and he gets the impression that he is being asked to walk into a loosebox.

As soon as a horse is in place he should be tied properly and the partitions secured, giving him enough room to stretch his legs and balance himself against the movement of the vehicle, particularly when cornering.

If horses can reach each other and squabble during the journey they will need sniffer boards or rack chains with quick-release clips. Sniffer boards are essential when fillies and colts or mares and stallions are being carried together.

Horses need good ventilation, but they should be kept out of draughts. Roof vents and roof spinners are very good providing they are positioned correctly, but they can get knocked off or become damaged when the horsebox is driven under the branches of trees or other low objects. Windows should always be of toughened glass and have protective metal grills where necessary.

There is no foolproof way of loading a difficult horse. It is mainly a matter of common sense and trying to work out whether the horse is just being bloody-minded, or whether there is something really worrying him.

Chapter 8

Horseboxes and the Law

Gross Weight and HGV Licences

All horseboxes are classed as 'goods vehicles' in that they are 'mechanically propelled vehicles constructed or adapted for the carriage of goods or burden'. Their gross weight will determine whether they are classified as a heavy motor car or a heavy goods vehicle.

If the gross weight is between 3.5 tonnes and 7.5 tonnes the horsebox may be driven by a person of 18 years of age or over who holds a full Group A driving licence. A gross weight in excess of 7.5 tonnes will mean that the horsebox is a heavy goods vehicle, and the driver will need to hold a Heavy Goods Driving Licence in addition to a Group A driving licence.

In calculating the gross weight of a vehicle towing a trailer the gross weight of the trailer must also be included, and thus an HGV licence may be required if the gross weight of both vehicles exceeds 7.5 tonnes.

There are various classes of Heavy Goods Vehicle Driving Licence. Vehicles which have two axles and four wheels will need a Class 3 HGV licence if they have an automatic or semi-automatic transmission. A rigid vehicle with more than two axles will need a Class 2 or a Class 2A licence according to the transmission. For licence purposes the twin wheels at each end of the axle count as a single wheel.

Horseboxes not exceeding 3.5 tonnes gross vehicle weight may be driven by anyone holding a car driving licence who is 17 years of age or over. Although those aged 18 or over may drive vehicles up to 7.5

tonnes, they must be 21 years of age or over to obtain a Heavy Goods Vehicle Licence. There is, however, a Young Heavy Goods Drivers Scheme where it is possible for people of 18 years of age or more to learn to drive Class 3 Heavy Goods Vehicles. As with towing vehicles generally, people with provisional licences are not allowed to drive any horsebox which is towing a trailer.

Obtaining an HGV licence requires an exceptionally high standard of driving, and professional advice and training is certainly to be recommended. A medical examination will be required before the provisional HGV licence is issued. The Ministry test usually lasts for about two hours and candidates have to demonstrate an advanced standard of vehicle handling in both on and off the road conditions. They also have to pass an oral examination on the Highway Code, and answer other questions on matters affecting the safety of the vehicle on which the test is being taken. Failure to pass is expensive, and there is no reduction in the fee for a re-test.

Dual Responsibility

There are two manufacturers involved in the manufacture of a horsebox. There is the manufacturer who designs and markets the chassis (including the engine and power train), and the specialist bodybuilder who designs and builds the body, and mounts it on a suitable chassis. Although the chassis manufacturer is responsible for the safety and design of the chassis and its components, it is the bodybuilder who must ensure that the finished horsebox conforms with all the legal regulations.

Plating

Vehicles which have an unladen weight of more than 1525kg (30cwt) must be tested annually at a Department of Transport Vehicle Testing Station, and application should be made on the correct form to the Swansea Headquarters at least a month before the test becomes due. The test for a commercial vehicle is known as plating because a plate is issued showing the unladen and gross vehicle weights, as well as the permitted axle loadings. The axle loadings are particularly important with a horsebox as the weight distribution may vary considerably according to the load. Correct balance is one of the secrets of good horsebox design, and a badly designed horsebox may break the law when unladen because the body alone may place too much weight on the front axle, and yet be within the law when the vehicle is carrying horses at the rear.

Horseboxes should have the weight marked on the nearside, and have the official plating certificate in the cab, usually fixed to the inside of the passenger door or the engine cover.

Each year the chassis, brakes, steering and other important aspects of the vehicle are carefully inspected and tested at the Testing Station, and owners would be wise to have their horseboxes thoroughly checked and the chassis steam cleaned beforehand.

Spot Checks

Apart from the annual inspection, all commercial vehicles are liable to undergo spot checks either during a journey or on the owner's own premises, to ensure that all the regulations are being obeyed.

The checks may be carried out by an authorised examiner from the Ministry of Transport, by certifying officers, or by a police officer in uniform. They will have the authority to issue an order GV9, prohibiting the vehicle from being used on the road until any defects have been rectified, or the load reduced if the vehicle is overweight. They may also issue a less serious order, GV219, which notifies the owner of minor defects requiring attention. If an examiner feels that the gross weight of the vehicle is being exceeded he has the authority to insist on its being taken to the nearest public weighbridge to be weighed complete with the driver, the load and all passengers. Refusal to comply can result in prosecution for both the driver and the vehicle owner.

When a spot check is being made the inspector will also look to see that the correct Road Fund Licence is being displayed and that it is not out of date.

Operator's Licences

An Operator's Licence ('O' Licence) is required for vehicles having a gross weight in excess of 3.5 tonnes, where the vehicle is used for hire and reward or in connection with a trade or business. Owners of horseboxes in excess of 3.5 tonnes gross vehicle weight who are not sure of their position with regard to Operator's Licences should seek the advice of their local Traffic Area.

There are two major types of 'O' Licence: standard licences which must be obtained when operating vehicles over 3.5 tonnes gross vehicle weight for hire and reward; and restricted licences which are needed for goods vehicles exceeding the gross weight when used to carry 'own account' goods. Restricted licences allow the holder to operate both in the UK and abroad. Standard licences are further subdivided into National only (allowing operation only in the UK), and National and International, which allows hire and reward operation in the UK and abroad.

All applicants for Operator's Licences must satisfy the Licensing Authority as to their previous conduct, maintenance facilities and arrangements, operating centre and finance. Applicants for standard

61

licences must either be 'professionally competent' themselves or employ a transport manager who meets this requirement.

Certain horseboxes may be classified as Farmers' Vehicles, and where they are used only for carrying that farmer's own produce and goods, and (on limited occasions only) the produce and goods of other farmers, they may apply for the concessionary rate of Excise duty. However, if the vehicle is used at any time for carrying anyone else's goods or produce, the full goods vehicle rate of duty will apply.

Owners of vehicle combinations used for the carriage of goods in connection with a trade or business must comply with operating licensing regulations. These regulations are the Transport Act 1968 (sections 60–94), the Road Traffic Act 1974 (section 16 and schedule 4), and the Goods Vehicles (Operator's Licences, Qualifications and Fees) Regulations 1984 (SI 1984 No 176).

Quite apart from the question of Operator's Licences, the rate of duty payable on each vehicle is determined by type, weight, and the use to which it is to be put. All these details have to be included in the application for registration and re-licensing, and as with all matters concerning Excise revenue there are heavy penalties if the owner is found guilty of failing to register or tax vehicles or for failing to pay the correct rate of tax.

Fortunately the majority of horseboxes are privately owned and used purely for pleasure, and may be taxed privately for the same cost as a private car.

Tachographs and Log Books

The United Kingdom and EEC regulations now in force require all goods-carrying vehicles which have a gross weight in excess of 3.5 tonnes to be fitted with a tachograph, and it is important to note that exemption from Operator's Licence requirements or Excise licensing has no bearing on the requirement to fit a tachograph.

A Department of Transport press notice issued on 29 June 1981 expressed the view that equestrian leisure pursuits were likely to be regarded in the courts as 'cultural events'. This would effectively exempt horseboxes exceeding 3.5 tonnes gross weight from the need for a tachograph, provided that they were used privately and that the rules regarding drivers' hours were observed. This relaxation would of course apply only in the United Kingdom, and would not be available to those vehicles being used to carry horses as part of a business operation.

The tachograph is an instrument fitted in place of, or in some cases in tandem with, the vehicle speedometer. It is required to be capable of recording the speed of the vehicle, the distance travelled, the time spent at the wheel (driving), the time spent on other work or activities, the time spent on breaks for rest and refreshment, rest time between working days, and each time that the tachograph is opened. The instrument must have a facility to allow the driver to examine that a satisfactory trace is being made on the chart without opening the instrument. It must also be possible with the instrument opened to examine the record of the previous nine hours without having to remove the chart.

All tachographs must be calibrated and sealed at an Approved Tachograph Centre, and the Traffic Area Office can supply the names of these centres. The regulations governing the fitting, calibration and use are in the EEC Council Regulations 1463/79 as amended, and the Passenger and Goods Vehicles (Recording) Regulations 1979 (S.1 1979 No 1746).

One-day courses on tachographs are available at most of the Road Transport Industry Training Board Heavy Goods Vehicle Training Centres; the Headquarters of the Board are at Capitol House, Empire Way, Wembley, Middlesex HA9 0NG, telephone: (01) 902 8880.

Tachographs are also the subject of seminars conducted by the Road Haulage Association and the Freight Transport Association.

A log book is not required when a tachograph is being used, but in cases when a log book may be used instead of a tachograph each driver will require a separate log book and be responsible for keeping his own daily record. Log books may be purchased from most leading stationers, and are quite simple to understand and use.

Speed Limits

On roads other than restricted roads or motorways, rigid goods vehicles with a maximum laden weight not exceeding 7.5 tonnes may travel at a maximum speed of 60mph on dual carriageways and 50mph on single carriageways (lower limits apply if a trailer is being towed as well). For rigid vehicles having a maximum laden weight exceeding 7.5 tonnes, the maximum speeds are 50mph on dual carriageways and 40mph on single carriageways.

On motorways rigid vehicles not exceeding 7.5 tonnes maximum laden weight are allowed to travel at a maximum of 70mph. Rigid vehicles exceeding 7.5 tonnes are limited to 60mph. Goods vehicles both above and below 7.5 tonnes are limited to 60mph on motorways when towing a trailer. Cars, car-derived vans and dual-purpose vehicles towing a trailer are limited to 50mph on all roads (unless a particular stretch of road is subject to a lower limit).

Towing Trailers

There are certain problems associated with coupling a trailer to a horsebox. It is likely that the trailer will be narrower than the horsebox, and will become lost from view in the mirrors more easily. The trailer can cause problems when a sharp bend or corner is being negotiated, even though a reasonably light trailer will have little effect, if any, on the general handling and behaviour of the much heavier towing vehicle.

Because the driver will have few reminders that he is towing a trailer, particular care must be taken and driving techniques must be modified. A lightweight trailer carrying, for example, a driving vehicle, will be particularly susceptible to cross winds, and turbulence and snaking may well occur. The advice given in Chapter 6 should be followed.

Lighting Requirements

Horseboxes must conform with the requirements of the Road Vehicle Lighting Regulations and must be equipped with the following minimum obligatory lights:

Two white front position lamps showing to the front.

Two headlamps, white or yellow, permanently dipped or fitted with a dipping device.

Two red rear position lamps.

Two red stop lamps, non-flashing, showing to the rear.

At least one illuminated rear number plate.

One red rear fog lamp.

Two red reflectors showing to the rear.

Flashing type indicators showing to the front and the rear.

All the lights must be clean and in good working condition at all times when the horsebox is on a public highway.

Certain vehicles and trailers must be fitted with amber side reflex reflectors. Vehicles over 6m in length first used on or after 1 April 1986 and those over 8m in length first used before that date must be fitted with these reflex reflectors, as must any trailers having a length in excess of 5m. At least two (or possibly more) amber reflectors must be fitted to each side of all those vehicles and trailers specified.

Marking

Apart from the plating certificate, and details as to weight, which must be painted on the chassis or bodywork, goods vehicles over 7.5 tonnes maximum gross weight and trailers of more than 3.5 tonnes maximum gross weight and up to 13m long must be fitted with rear reflecting marker boards showing red fluorescent and yellow reflective diagonal stripes.

Vehicles and combinations more than 13m in length must be fitted with rear marker boards with the words 'LONG VEHICLE' in black lettering on a yellow reflective background with a red fluorescent border. The marker boards should carry the marking 'BS AU 152–1970'. There are different types of each marker board to accommodate the construction of the vehicle.

Maintenance

In addition to the vehicle manufacturer's recommended servicing, which is designed to maintain the horsebox in a roadworthy condition, drivers are required to keep up the bodywork and interior in accordance with the regulations governing the type of load carried.

Where horses and ponies are concerned, this maintenance includes the cleaning and disinfecting of the body, and examining the walls, floor and partitions for general condition and damage. The regulations are drafted to ensure as far as possible the safe, healthy transit of the animals and must be complied with at all times.

Regulations

Horseboxes are required to comply with the Motor Vehicles (Construction and Use) Regulations which, as their title implies, is concerned with the construction, mechanical condition, and the use of the vehicle. Drivers must also be aware of the additional regulations which apply according to the type of load being carried on each journey. The regulations are the Transit of Horses Order 1951 (S1. 1951 No 335) and the Transit of Animals Order 1931, S.R. and O. 1931 No 750.

Chapter 9

Choosing a Horsebox

Construction

The effect of EEC regulations, the need for more owners to transport their valuable horses over long distances, and the obvious advantages of overnight accommodation in the one vehicle, have all had a beneficial effect on horsebox design and construction in recent years.

Wood and aluminium have in many cases given way to modern plastics, which are tougher, safer and more hygienic, and in some cases easier to repair and less expensive to maintain. Where weight is such an important factor, particularly with non-HGV models, the new GRP (glass-reinforced plastic) materials can offer considerable savings, and they also enable the latest building techniques to be used, so saving construction time and increasing efficiency. There has also been a radical new approach to flooring, with rubber-based compounds which are hardwearing and will seal a floor to prevent the leakage of urine, which might otherwise offend against regulations when the vehicle is used on board ships.

In choosing a horsebox, whatever the size or class of vehicle a customer is looking for, much the same basic qualities will have to be considered. Visual appearance and attention to detail will obviously be important, because they will be a rough guide to the overall quality and finish. A poor exterior finish may well reflect a serious lack of attention to detail elsewhere.

Although the different materials used for the exterior bodywork may all have individual advantages or drawbacks, the final choice could be largely a matter of individual preference, or purely incidental to the price and type of vehicle required. It should be remembered, however, that most horseboxes have to stand out in all types of weather, and freedom from rust and rot or high maintenance costs can be very important. Strength and safety are of paramount importance.

Interior Fittings

Interior fittings must be robust and firmly secured. While all bolts and latches must be sturdy and positive in location, they must also be easy to operate.

Partitions must be strong enough to bear the weight of a large horse, and extend at least from ground to shoulder height. They should be smooth and preferably well padded. Although many horses will travel quite well with narrow partitions some distance from the floor, accidents can happen through no fault of the horsebox or its driver, and if a horsebox gets tilted off its wheels the horses can slip below the partitions and get trampled on by the other occupants. Strong partitions to ground level can help prevent this happening.

Sniffer boards can also prevent horses from getting to each other and they are essential when colts and fillies have to travel together in the same area of the horsebox. Higher partitions are also a benefit because they do prevent horses from seeing too much of each other when travelling side by side.

Breast straps must be strong enough to bear the weight of the horse and should also have easy-to-operate catches which can be opened when required despite the weight and pressure of a horse.

Breast bars should preferably be padded and at the correct height to give the horse maximum protection. They can be left open below or filled in with grooms' doors. It is mainly a matter of preference.

Horses need plenty of headroom and the minimum permitted height is 7ft. In some cases that can be rather on the low side and good head padding will be required.

Position of Horses

The travelling position of the horses is also to a certain extent a matter of preference. Some people insist on forward facing stalls, and there are others who claim that horses travel more comfortably when facing towards the rear. Diagonal stalls have also become very popular, particularly where owners wish to have a horsebox which is below the 7.5 tonnes gross vehicle weight HGV Licence limit and has the ability to carry four large horses and provide luxury living accommodation. In those cases forward-facing stalls would not be possible because of the additional length and thus weight required, and a compromise has to be reached. Some of the horse area has to be sacrificed in order to allow for a larger living area.

Most partitions are now made adjustable to allow for different stall widths, and horses needing more room can usually be catered for. Certainly the size of the stall and horse area, stall configuration, the provision of feed bins and tack boxes, hay/rug racks, and additional water containers, can all be tailored to customer requirements and specification at a price. Most manufacturers have a standard range of horseboxes, and costs will increase when customers wish to go outside the standard model specifications. It should be appreciated, however, that almost all horsebox manufacturers base the design of their horseboxes on years of experience of trying to cater for a wide range of requirements. The wise manufacturers end up with a range of safe and comfortable horse transporters which will suit the majority of their customers because they are the best compromise, taking into account size, weight, performance and price.

Ramps

Ramps need to be strong enough to stand the weight of a large horse, and as some horses load better than others, the ramp may have to bear the weight of a horse jumping on to it. Although some owners don't like the ramp to be too steep, there are others, equally experienced, who feel horses will load better up a steep ramp, providing there are no large steps to be negotiated at the top. Humans seem to be concerned with the steepness of a ramp more often than the horses, particularly if the ramp covering becomes slippery. The choice of covering usually rests between matting with wooden slats, or rubber with aluminium slats. Some manufacturers are now using products such as Granilastic which they also use on the floor of the horse area. Rubber will wear better than matting but it needs to be ribbed or it will become rather slippery in wet weather.

It is important that ramps can be raised and lowered easily and that they don't become too heavy. All ramps have some form of assistance either in the form of springs or, in the case of some modern horseboxes, adjustable torsion bars.

Cab and Living Accommodation

Access from the cab to the horses during transit is considered by most owners to be highly desirable, not only as a safety measure but also to enable rugs to be checked and horses to be fed and watered without stopping during a journey. If the horsebox has living accommodation at the front there is a door leading from the living and tack area through into the horse stalls.

Living accommodation can range from the bare essentials to luxury features which will include showers, flush toilets, air conditioning, stereo, video and colour television.

Customers would be wise to remember that the old adage about getting what you pay for applies as much to horseboxes as to anything else.

Types of horsebox

Horseboxes may be designed to carry horses facing forwards, facing backwards, or loaded diagonally, and many manufacturers will fit out a box to meet a customer's individual needs (including living accommodation). Illustrated here are just three of the many permutations possible.

Box designed to carry four to six horses facing forwards.

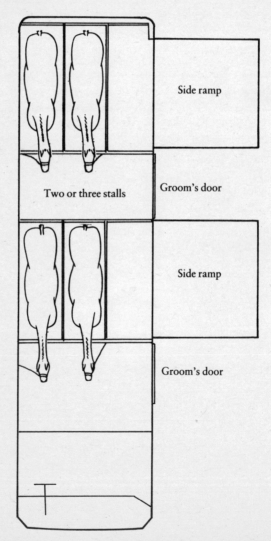

Side ramp

Two or three stalls

Groom's door

Side ramp

Groom's door

Four- or five-horse box, two
horses facing forwards, two or
three horses facing the rear.

Box designed to carry five or six
horses loaded diagonally, and with living
accommodation at the front.

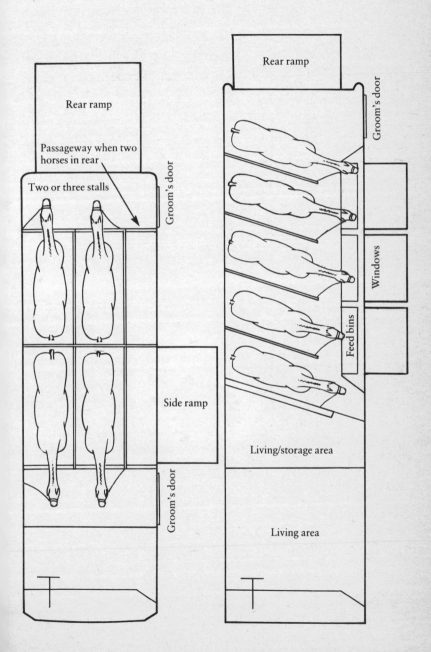

Chapter 10

Insurance

In the United Kingdom it is a legal requirement for the user of any horsebox on the road to be insured by an authorised insurer, who is a member of the Motor Insurers' Bureau, against liability law, against death, compensation for injury caused by another person, and the cost of emergency medical treatment for all parties resulting from an accident.

All passengers must be covered, as in the case of every other motor vehicle, because an 'own risk' agreement cannot be made between the owner, the driver or the passengers.

The minimum insurance coverage is the 'third party' policy which provides for the basic legal requirements, along with coverage against claims for any damage caused to property belonging to third parties. The limit of these claims is normally £50,000 per accident, but that sum may be increased by the payment of an additional premium which also usually includes fire and theft.

The main drawback with the third party policy is the fact that it does not cover the cost of repairs to the insured person's own vehicle. The high cost of repairs makes it almost essential to have a 'fully comprehensive' insurance policy for expensive vehicles like a horsebox, so that damage repair costs can be covered.

The contents of every insurance policy should be read very carefully because most policies carry a list of exclusions for which claims cannot be met.

These exclusions usually include:

Depreciation, wear and tear, mechanical or electrical breakdown. Damage to tyres through braking, punctures, cuts or bursts.

Death, injury or damage caused when off the road during loading or unloading, and caused by any person other than the driver or attendant of the vehicle.

Manslaughter defence costs, although these can usually be covered for an additional premium.

Damage to any bridge, weighbridge, road, or anything beneath the road, caused either by the weight of the vehicle or by any vibration caused by the vehicle.

Insurance policies do not automatically provide coverage for loss of earnings, drivers' wages or the cost of hiring a replacement vehicle if a vehicle is rendered unusable due to an accident. Such cover can be arranged, however, by the payment of an additional premium.

In the case of a horsebox it is also particularly important to establish exactly what insurance coverage is provided for death or injury to any animals being transported.

Horsebox owners who are transporting animals on behalf of customers must first establish what is known as 'Conditions of Carriage', and arrange a 'Goods in Transit' insurance in accordance with the conditions which have been agreed.

Many transport operators adopt the 'Conditions of Carriage' which have been compiled by the Road Haulage Association. In such cases the conditions must be made known to all customers and owners of horses being transported, and should also be referred to on all invoices and business notepaper.

Details of load insurance coverage are contained in the Conditions of Carriage, and it is the responsibility of the customer to demand additional or increased coverage and for the carrier to arrange the extra coverage with his insurer.

It should be remembered that policies are usually declared null and void if the insured vehicles are not maintained in a roadworthy and safe condition. The same applies if the driver is not correctly licensed to drive the vehicle.

In checking insurance coverage it is wise to make sure that the policy includes any trailer and its contents which may be towed by the vehicle. The small print should be studied very carefully because the financial costs of an accident with a horsebox which may be carrying valuable horses can be very high.

Chapter 11

Accident Procedure

The increased volume of traffic on the roads has also meant an increase in the number of accidents, and unfortunately the number of incidents involving horses and horse transport is also high.

The course of action taken by the driver of a vehicle involved in an accident can have a considerable bearing not only on the apportionment of blame but also on any possible prosecution proceedings, and it is important for all drivers to be aware of their legal obligations.

An accident can be said to have occurred where, through the presence of a vehicle, damage or injury is caused to a person or persons, certain domestic animals, or to property on or adjacent to a road.

DOs

Providing a driver has not been seriously injured and is capable of action the wisest course to follow would be to:

Stop. This is a legal requirement because it is an offence not to do so after an accident.

Arrange traffic control. This measure may be necessary if there is traffic congestion, and it should prevent further accidents, and help to avoid unwanted onlookers.

Take any necessary fire precautions. Any outbreak of fire should of course be dealt with as far as possible before the arrival of the fire brigade, but even if fire has not broken out it would be wise to ensure that the ignition is switched off and the batteries are disconnected. Any spillage of fuel should be covered with sand or earth, and people should be warned not to smoke in the area.

Check any injuries and carry out emergency first aid. There is advice on what to do at the back of the Highway Code, but first aid training can be of tremendous help. Drivers would be well advised to know how to put an injured person into the recovery position, how to give the kiss of life, how to stop heavy bleeding, and how to make an injured person more comfortable before professional medical help arrives. The correct course of action taken quickly after an accident can save a life or prevent further serious injury.

Call the necessary emergency services. The course of action to be taken will depend on the seriousness of the accident. The police should be notified, and if necessary the fire and ambulance services should be called to the scene. The person making the calls should be fully aware of the exact location of the accident, and the number of people injured. If horses or other animals are involved it may also be necessary to call a veterinary surgeon.

Exchange particulars with anyone else involved in the accident. In an accident a driver is required by law to give his name and address, along with insurance details if personal injury is involved, to the other driver and to any person who may have reasonable grounds for requiring them. If for any reason a driver is unable to exchange these details, and if the police are not present, the driver must notify the police as soon as possible, or at least within 24 hours of the accident. A driver who is not able to produce evidence of insurance will be required to produce the insurance certificate at a designated police station within five days. This course of action is a legal requirement, but as long as no one is injured and the drivers of the vehicles exchange all the necessary particulars, the accident need not be reported to the police.

Get statements from any reliable witnesses present. The first essential is to obtain names and addresses and if possible telephone numbers. People may be in a hurry and unwilling to stay long enough to give a statement; their memories are usually much clearer, however, if they can be persuaded to give an on-the-spot statement. If that is not possible, a statement can always be obtained later.

Examine the vehicles involved. It is also wise to have one's own vehicle examined for roadworthiness following a serious accident before driving it away.

Make notes. It is important to gather as much information as possible about the scene of the accident, including location, names and dimensions of road, road markings, the position and type of any road signs, the position of vehicles before and after the accident and their estimated speeds, the position and length of any skid marks, the road surface, weather and visibility at the time of the accident. A sketch of the scene can be very useful when filling in an accident report later.

Obtain permission to leave the scene of the accident. If any police are present a driver is legally required to ask their permission before leaving.

Inform the owner. Anyone driving someone else's vehicle should give them details of the accident as soon as possible so that they in turn can inform their own insurance company.

The procedure taken will of course depend on the seriousness of the accident and whether anyone has been injured. In all circumstances it is important to know what to do as the driver of a vehicle involved.

DON'Ts

A driver should also know what *not* to do:

Do not admit liability. No matter how guilty a driver may feel as to the cause of an accident it is important never to admit liability. Far better to wait until a solicitor can be consulted and the full facts concerning the accident are made known. A driver who admits liability has no case to offer.

Do not make any statements at the time. It is not generally known that a driver is not even required to make a statement to the police at the scene of the accident, and may wait until legal advice has been sought, or at least until he has recovered from the shock of the accident and can think more clearly.

A driver should also never delay in informing the insurance company and letting them have the full facts as soon as possible.

The British Horse Society will supply excellent accident report forms to anyone who has had an accident involving horses. Accidents involving horses are currently averaging eight a day in the United Kingdom and the information contained in the report forms will enable the Society to gather statistics which can be of considerable help in moulding future legislation towards safeguarding the horse, the rider and the driver.

Apart from the normal emergency services there is also an emergency scheme for horses. Details are available from the British Horse Society at the British Equestrian Centre, Stoneleigh, Kenilworth, Warwickshire CV8 2LR, telephone: Coventry (0203) 52241 (10 lines).

There is no substitute for safe driving. It is hoped that readers of this book will be in a better position to safeguard their own welfare, as well as ensuring that the horses under their care travel safely and in as much comfort as possible, and that accidents are not caused through ignorance or negligence.

Index